Landing On Venus:

Finding fate in your next date
Or finding happiness in your wife and your life

Harry Allen Strunk

Cover Illustration by Marvin Paracuelles

To order additional copies of this book, contact:
Xlibris Corporation
1-888-795-4274
www.Xlibris.com
Orders@Xlibris.com
125629

To the women in my life

Landing on Venus *honors the magnificence of feminine energy in the universe; whether it manifests itself in the fierceness of the mighty Grizzly bear protecting her cubs, the courage draped around the Statute of Liberty lighting the way, or the loving tender embrace we absorbed as small infants nestled in our mother's arms. What would the world be without wives and mothers, sisters and daughters, grandmothers and granddaughters?*

Landing on Venus *is dedicated to all of the wonderful women in the world; especially my wife Patty who has blessed me for 38 remarkable years; my mother Norma who follows me around every day even though I can no longer see her; and my sister Julie who magnifies the mysteries of Venus. Last but not least is my 14-year assistant Pat who has a wonderful literary mind and perseveres through my writing process at times when not many would. The bottom line is they all put up with me and for that I am very blessed.*

Foreword to Landing on Venus

Why a book called *"Landing on Venus: Finding fate in your next date or happiness in your wife and your life"*?

Life is imperfect and so are relationships. It's irrelevant to argue about who is to blame or whether the divorce was in the best interests of all involved. What is important is the devastation divorces can cause and the impact they can have not only on the participants, but the children who are often held hostage.

Within my family of parents and siblings, there have been six marriages and only two of those have been successful to date. That percentage is probably worse than the national average. I was hit with the full fury of divorce when my parents separated after 28 years of marriage. A friend of mine made the comment that at least I was an adult when my parents divorced and I didn't have to go through it when I was a child. No matter the age, it hurts. Over time I've observed other divorces wreak havoc on my sister, brother, nieces, nephews, in-laws, and friends.

If this book can help avoid just one divorce and the consequences for that family, then writing it was worth it.

Why a Landing on Venus workshop?

It occurred to me after this book was written that readership in America continues to decline. Men are busy with endeavors other than reading and yet they yearn to discuss issues amongst themselves when the opportunity presents itself. What better topic to discuss than marriages and female relationships?

I was pleasantly surprised when the first bible study group I approached agreed to become my test case. With twelve men in attendance, I couldn't shut them up. The experience of starting a snowball rolling and watching it gain momentum was very gratifying. Hearing firsthand the wisdom and experience of men who have been married 65 years, 58 years, 52 years . . . is simply impossible to replicate but maybe these elders could help younger men just starting out with female relationships or in their marriages?

Finally, another reason to do workshops is because writing is a lonely endeavor and can be isolating. Interaction with others regarding my past writing and ideas is very stimulating. These workshops help to keep me engaged in my daily writing and provide a sense that my writing may be of significance. For a free workshop contact me at landingvenus@gmail.com or go to the website to view projects in process at *www.aspengrovepublishing.com*.

How to use Landing on Venus?

Part One is a section of ideas gathered from friends over time. This is a reference section for your use and further review on a regular basis when searching for approaches to making your Venus happy and your relationship productive and healthy.

Part Two consists of seven chapters used by me during my journey of self-discovery. Perhaps you may be able to use some of the chapters to better understand the most important person in your life—yourself!

> *"There are three things extremely hard, steel, a diamond, and to know one's self."*—**Benjamin Franklin**

Disclaimer

My testimony and confession

Anthony Robbins is a man I both admire and respect. His zeal for self-discovery, self-knowledge, and the willingness to share it is second to none. In fact his success has made him very wealthy. Yet, perhaps, it has also made him poor at the same time.

A few years ago when his marriage of 19 years came unraveled, he was attacked unmercifully for being a hypocrite. How could he be the guru of relationships in print, audio, and video and still get divorced?

He could because he's a male. He could because he's from Mars and, most importantly, because he is human. So am I. The greatest talent I possess when it comes to keeping my marriage intact and my wife happy is dumb luck.

I don't do all the things discussed in *Landing on Venus*. Sometimes, unfortunately, I don't do any of them at all. But that doesn't mean I don't keep trying and that's one reason I wrote them down . . . so I can remember!

Like most of us, I get up in the morning, make my mistakes, try to correct them, hopefully learn from them, and then LET THEM GO. Forgiving yourself is the first part of the Golden Rule—Love your neighbor as you love <u>yourself</u>.

Another great relationship book, *The Love Dare*, states it beautifully: Treat a woman the right way and she blooms, if you don't she will wilt. If the ideas presented here don't bloom for you or I someday become divorced, hopefully you will forgive me. In the meantime, I wish you all the best in one of the most profound journeys you will have in life . . . a marriage or significant intimacy with someone from Venus.

—Harry Allen Strunk

Landing on Venus:
Finding fate in your next date
Or happiness in your wife and your life

Table of contents

Introduction: Landing On Venus... 1

PART ONE—A Reference Book of Ideas 5

   Mission Contol: Going into orbit 7
   Communications: Calling command central............................ 9
   Morning: Blast off to a great new day 10
   Evening: Land on a happy note... 10
   Write/Music: Awaken those creative juices 12
   Outdoors: Play and grow together 13
   Traveling: Discover new worlds 13
   Birthdays: Celebrate the essence of life................................ 14
   Anniversaries: Launch into special memories, places, and events.... 15
   Valentine's Day: Find Cupid among the stars 15
   Christmas: Give back to the universe.................................... 16
   Advanced Ideas: Boldly go where few men have gone before 16

PART TWO—Chapters of Self-discovery 19

Chapter One
   Lining up the stars: Honesty in dating..............................21
     Spiritual Exploration, Intellectual Compatibility,
     Hobbies and Outside Interests, Sex

Chapter Two
   All systems go: Healthy marriage attitudes;...................33
     They can change over time

Chapter Three
   Come in mission control: What do you ask for?...........38
     Courage + Strength + Wisdom + Humility + Patience = Compassion

Chapter Four
   Straight and level flight: Balancing happiness 48
   Exercise, Work, Social, Solitude

Chapter Five
   Meteor showers ahead: Embracing obsession 58
   Rid yourself of negative thoughts

Chapter Six
   Truth in the universe: The Golden Rule 68
   Common theme in religions and disciplines

Chapter Seven
   Freedom of Space: Spacious Skies 72
   Short story about spiritual freedom

Introduction

Landing On Venus

This book landed in your hands for a reason. There are no coincidences in life. You are about to embark on a trip into discovering more about yourself and that special woman in your life.

I wrote this book so that I might be nicer to my wife. Not 80 percent of the time or 90 percent of the time but 99.9 percent of the time. I don't often reach that goal but I'm coming closer all the time and I think this book can help you too.

Men are from Mars, women are from Venus.

This John Gray book title may best explain the number of divorces in this country today. Is anyone astonished that marriages often crash upon the rocks of despair in today's high tech society where distractions keep couples from having honest, deep connecting conversations? A world where it is easier to type an email than pick up the phone; where texting, Facebook, and Twitter compete with meaningful dialogue.

Studying the art of a good marriage and an intimate relationship is not a national past time. It is not taught in schools and religious education usually falls woefully short. Finding an effective marriage counselor can be difficult and may not always help to nurture a healthy loving partnership.

People brush their teeth, have regular medical checkups and buy health club memberships as preventive maintenance. But where do we find a preventive program to maintain a healthy marriage and avoid divorce?

As men in today's complex world, the answer might be right in front of our noses. KISS does not represent something that occurs right before our favorite extracurricular activity. It stands for: Keep It Simple Stupid.

In reviewing your dating era, which might seem like ancient history for some of you, some of the simplest and silliest efforts on your part are probably what your wife remembers most today. They can become the cement that bonds the cracks and fissures that appear in your marriage over time. It could be that those occasions were the most heartfelt and honest of the relationship.

Some of the ideas listed here might seem trivial or unimportant. Remember that life on Venus is much different than Mars. Your Venus may view television sports, hunting, fishing, and other manly pursuits on Mars as intergalactic, trivial or, at the very least, unimportant.

Past visitors to Venus have found KISS to be invaluable. They have followed their boyish childhood intuition and have completed many successful missions when visiting Venus. They have magnified the love in their connection with their best friend; their wife or significant other.

And something interesting happens when you take the time to show that special woman affection. It attracts her affection and love to you in return, just like a magnet.

So in reading the following ideas, be aware that you are taking them in through your eyes and into your mind. Many ideas will not resonant and thus fail to germinate from within. But those few gems, the ideas that inspire and encourage you to be the best husband and best friend that you can be, will eventually come back out driven by your heart; expressed through love and tenderness.

Hang on to this book, take notes in the back, and try to do something special with your Venus on a regular basis. Remember; show her the simplest compassion and affection possible. Be sincere. Be aware. You just might be amazed with the results.

PART ONE

A Reference Book of Ideas

MISSION CONTOL: Going into orbit

Ask her what a perfect weekend would look like and then put that weekend into place.

Tell her you are having a "Mary Day" (or Judy Day, or Jane Day, whatever your wife's name). Do everything she wants you to do for the day.

Take her to lunch during the week.

Wash and vacuum her car. Doing it yourself says something extra.

Buy her a new nightgown or swimsuit.

Clean the entire refrigerator out and include dusting the top and sweeping under it.

Say you are sorry and what your faults were in the disagreement. Be sincere and offer some way to be of service or make up that is acceptable to her.

While she is taking a shower, warm a towel in the dryer and give it to her when she is finished.

Tell her something you appreciate about her every day for a week.

Wink at her when you are with friends or in public.

Hold her hand in public.

Hold her hand at weddings.

Give her a hug when she cries.

Ask her to hold you when you cry. Don't be afraid to cry in front of her.

Clean her reading glasses for her with a special polishing cloth or cleaning patch.

Take her to the jewelry store of her choice and let her buy something she likes.

Buy clothes for her and put them away in her closet for a surprise when she finds them later.

Do a volunteer service project together.

Approach her class reunion with enthusiasm and interest. Talk to her past classmates and do something to make the weekend special for her such as take photos and make a photo album afterwards.

Give her a framed picture of the two of you.

Get her a mug or T-shirt with the two of you and/or the kids' picture(s) on it.

Remind her of her accomplishments by getting a shirt from her high school or college. Talk about things she has accomplished.

Clean and organize the entire garage when she is away. Amaze and stun her.

Ask her one thing that you do that annoys her and then try to avoid doing it.

If you live in a winter climate, write a huge I love you in the snow.

Make her a snow man carrying a bouquet of flowers. Make a snow man and snow woman with a heart around them. Make a snow angel and put her name beside it.

Write love notes to her on her iced-over car window.

Pray for her and your intimacy.

Offer to help her if she has a special charity, fundraiser or outside interest.

Ask her thoughts and wishes before making donations.

COMMUNICATIONS: Calling command central

Record her number first in your speed dial at work and on your cell phone.

Try not to take calls from others while talking with her on the phone.

Call her back immediately when you have to interrupt a call with her.

Call her during the day to just say "hi" and check how her day is going.

Leave a message on her voice mail listing all the reasons you love her so much.

Send her an email from work that tells her how much she means to you.

Begin statements with "I feel" rather than "I think".

Tell her how beautiful and special she is.

Tell her she looks like she has lost weight, but only if it does look that way.

Take time to tell her how nice her new haircut or manicure looks.

Praise her publicly for her strengths, character, and abilities.

Give her compliments in front of the children.

Discuss your children and ask how you can help.

Share your goals and dreams with her. Ask her to share her dreams.

Ask for her opinion on things (politics, people, life).

MORNING: Blast off to a great new day

Buy a helium theme balloon from the local grocery store. For instance get a pink dolphin with a sign that says "I flip over you." These vinyl custom balloons can float around for up to three weeks on a single fill.

Have a cup of hot tea or coffee ready for her when she gets to the kitchen.

Serve her breakfast in bed.

Make it a regular routine to give her a hug and a kiss before you leave in the morning. Wish her a wonderful day.

Take a special picture of the two of you and put it on her bathroom mirror before she gets up in the morning.

Leave a love note with her toothbrush.

Let her know what time you will be returning home and then make that a priority by being on time. Call her if you will be delayed.

Ask what her favorite radio station is so you can tune the clock radio to that station when she wakes up in the morning. Also program it into the car she drives.

EVENING: Land on a happy note

Surprise her by asking her out for a "date" just like the old days. Don't tell her where you are going; keep her in suspense. That is half the fun!

Cook her a candlelight dinner, serve it to her, and wash the dishes afterward. If this is outside your talent level, hire a caterer to come in and serve dinner.

Compliment her cooking. Help clean the dishes.

Unload the dishwasher and put everything away.

Check with her before you invite anyone to dinner.

Take a cooking or wine tasting class together.

Buy red and white roses, separate the petals, and spread them across the bed before retiring for the evening.

If you live in a cold climate and have a fireplace, lay out her pajamas in front of the fire prior to bedtime so they are warm and cozy.

Lie on her side of the bed and have it warm before she retires for the evening.

Buy a new pillowcase. Write "I Love You" on it with permanent marker.

Never argue in the bedroom.

Give her a massage with fragranced body oils. If you are really courageous, give her a hot rock massage but get directions first and perhaps practice on someone! Also there are certain kinds of roller pins and rolling wheels that work great on backs and legs.

Share the highlights of your day with her while she is preparing dinner.

Spend an evening together looking at family movies and/or family picture albums.

When receiving a fortune cookie, always say it reads "You have a beautiful and wonderful wife."

Count to ten while you kiss her when you come home from work.

Hang up your clothes and put away your own laundry.

Watch a sunset together.

Do something active like putting together a jigsaw puzzle.

WRITE/MUSIC: Awaken those creative juices

Write a story about your dating courtship that recounts how you felt about her and the circumstances surrounding your falling in love.

Determine the meaning behind her name and find an appropriate depiction over the Internet. Frame it for her.

Leave a love note in a book you know she is reading.

Make a list of all of her great qualities and share it with her. You can do this using letters of the alphabet from A to Z, i.e., **A**lways there for me. **B**eautiful beyond description. **C**ares about our family, etc.

Help her write a year-end letter to friends and family.

Write her a poem or love letter.

Get her and yourself diaries and regularly write about a common subject. Exchange diaries after you both are done writing. Explain unclear statements and concepts to each other. This could provide a great gift for your grandchildren to read someday.

Record a CD of all of your special songs together such as wedding songs, favorite dance songs and special event music that reminds you of each other. A great gift for you as well!

Go to the music store and pick the titles of 10 songs that express your love for her. Reprint those song titles and give it to her.

Contact the local newspaper from her hometown and have them send her a subscription.

Find her favorite movie and buy her the DVD. Watch it together.

Find her favorite music group and buy her the album. Take her to the group's concert if available in your area.

If you have a piano, buy a piano player with her favorite music.

OUTDOORS: Play and grow together

Buy a tandem bicycle so you can ride together around the neighborhood.

Learn to play golf together so you can have time in the golf cart away from others.

Don't compete intensely in sports against one another. Play for fun.

Praise her sports ability when around others.

Go for a walk or hike together and stay at the same pace.

Plant and maintain a garden together. Include flowers that you can dazzle her with later.

Arrange a lunch and take her on a picnic.

TRAVELING: Discover new worlds

Open the car door and other doors for her.

Make sure you always arrive at the airport to pick her up before she arrives. Greet her with a bouquet of flowers.

Call her on an airline phone just to tell her you miss her.

Call her every night you are on the road.

Take her with you on business trips.

Get an emergency kit for her car. Keep tires and the car in safe condition. Join an emergency motor service that will provide roadside assistance when she calls.

Revisit somewhere special that you went such as on your honeymoon.

After she packs her suitcase, re-open it and place a love note inside telling her how much you miss her already.

BIRTHDAYS: Celebrate the essence of life

Search the newspaper archives or library and get the front page of the day she was born.

On her birthday, send flowers to your mother-in-law with a card thanking her for delivering such a special person into your life.

Fill the entire house with helium balloons on her birthday or your anniversary.

Host a special birthday party with friends where you have a Trivial Pursuit game made up from all of the little details from her past life. Separate them into different categories such as sports, friends, hobbies, children, family, etc.

Host a surprise birthday party with a theme such as casino night where you bring in gaming tables and guests can win/buy prizes at the end of the night.

Buy her a best selling book or one that she hasn't read yet from her favorite author.

Post a happy birthday sign in the front yard.

Give her a card with a copy of her baby picture from her family album letting her know she is your special baby.

ANNIVERSARIES: Launch into special memories, places, and events

Never forget your anniversary or her birthday. Write it in red ink on your new calendar each year. Remind yourself with a Dec. 31 note to place these dates into next year's calendar.

Make a collage of pictures from all of the special events in your life.

Buy a separate gift for each year of marriage on your anniversary and hide them throughout the house wrapped separately and each with a loving card, i.e. for 10 years of marriage you give her 10 presents.

Renew your wedding vows before an official with or without friends and family.

Talk about your first meeting date and when you knew you were first in love with her.

Visit the place where you first met. Go on the anniversary day of the first meeting.

Find a picture from your wedding day and place it where she will see it.

Make a huge anniversary banner and hang it across the family room to celebrate with her.

VALENTINE'S DAY: Find Cupid among the stars

Ask her if she will be your Valentine.

If you have a dog, design a huge heart of cardboard with a hole cut out to put around its neck with the words "Can I be your valentine?" She will know who it's from.

Buy a gold fish bowl with fish and floating hearts in the water.

Bring her home a giant Valentine's Day card that you have made from poster board.

Buy six valentines on Valentine's Day. Give one on that day and mail one to her every month for the next six months.

Go to a bath and accessories store and buy her a basket of sample shampoos, creams, lotions and conditioners or check the many companies that offer such an assortment on the Internet.

CHRISTMAS: Give back to the universe

Put mistletoe throughout the entire house during the holidays and take the opportunity to use it with her; kissing under the mistletoe.

Get a Christmas song album, make hot chocolate and spend a night together talking about past Christmas times.

Look at past family Christmas pictures and/or movies.

Take her on a hayrack ride or sleigh ride, complete with blankets and hot chocolate.

Take her Christmas caroling.

Volunteer together to deliver gifts to less fortunate families.

ADVANCED IDEAS: Boldly go where few men have gone before

Paint her toenails for her.

Massage her scalp—they sell special wiry tools for that—and comb her hair.

Buy a motorcycle with a helmet intercom system so you can have conversations away from other distractions while riding.

Get a boat that is comfortable and can be anchored out for getaway times together.

Buy a video camera and take family movies of important events.

Learn an instrument and play her favorite song for her during a special event in your lives. If you are brave, sing the words along with the song!

Hire a limo to pick you up for an unexpected date and pick up friends along the way to dinner to help celebrate a night out.

Take ballroom dance lessons together.

Hire a masseuse to come to the house and give her a massage.

Arrange an unexpected getaway for her to spend a weekend together with her best friend or relative.

PART TWO

Chapters of Self-discovery

"When men and women are able to respect and accept the differences then love has a chance to blossom."

—John Gray

Chapter One

Lining up the stars: Honesty in dating

What would you say to a young couple getting married today or in a relationship? What would your advice be to the young man?

These questions garnered some great advice at a Landing on Venus workshop, including such suggestions as in-depth communication, leading by example, humility, maintaining individuality and the need to recognize an equal partnership.

"If you put more into a relationship than you take out, then it will be successful," said one of the men. "There will be plenty of times when you have to take out more than you put in because of life circumstances. Getting ahead in the game by putting more in now will help during those times when you need to take out. If both are taking out, the relationship will fall apart."

For many single men today, sex is the driving force when they are looking for a relationship. It is the first thing they seek in deciding whether there is compatibility and whether they wish to go forward. Too often dating priorities might be listed in this order:

1. Sex
2. Hobbies and outside interests
3. Intellectual compatibility
4. Spiritual exploration

To foster a healthier intimacy, the opposite order of development seems reasonable:

1. Spiritual exploration
2. Intellectual compatibility
3. Hobbies and outside interests
4. Sex

Several participants at a workshop had been married more than 50 years. It is this kind of life experience from men willing to share some of their wisdom that can make a real difference in helping today's young couples. Mentoring was much more prevalent in the past century where tribal living and small communities made it much easier for elders to share knowledge with their young men. If we can recreate some of those mentoring opportunities, maybe men can lead the way in nurturing relationships.

So what's love got to do with it?

Dating is an attitude. When the motives are misplaced, they can create disastrous consequences for both parties involved. It is this process of vulnerability between two people that exposes their human soul and entrusts it to the other person. A mistreated soul can be very fragile. But if we approach the sacredness of dating and marriage with the dignity and honor it deserves, then our souls can remain healthy and intact.

Dating brings the heart into play—"I was just following my heart." But it is more than that because a heart can be misled and deceived. We should lead from our heart after first investing time and effort into that which our heart desires. The bible states, *for where your treasure is, there your heart will be also.*

Men and women share a unique responsibility when they enter a sexual encounter—there is the possibility of one or both being hurt through a failed intimacy. Look at sex as a sacred spiritual union and one of the most intimate means of sharing in the universe. Then a more sincere and sensitive connection will develop.

With women sex may or may not be the driving force, but they often seem to desire a more extensive experience of sharing and understanding their partner before having sex.

Within the singles dating world are Internet services that list a wide range of categories in determining the perfect dating match. These sites give you the opportunity to check off the boxes to determine the perfect partner. We should all know by now that there is no "perfect" partner because a relationship is like a garden . . . it has to be constantly maintained through nurturing and weeding, which equates to communication, understanding, and forgiveness.

Showing all your cards

Too often the initial courting and dating period can be a misleading and deceitful process. During most endeavors in life we wish to show our best side and put our best foot forward. How much time do we spend in the mirror checking our appearance before we go out on a date?

Presenting personal strengths and attributes during first introductions is fine. First impressions are important. But as two people start to create a bond, one that cultivates trust and respect, it is necessary to reveal and review each other's perceived shortcomings in a safe and nurturing manner. Creating the foundation and environment for such an exchange early on is what enhances a long lasting partnership.

Many dating couples today are too insecure to show their weaker side. They think they may lose their partner in the process. Others feel it just takes too much time and energy to discuss what they perceive as negativity. Some aren't even aware of, deny, or hide the parts of themselves they don't like or don't wish to share. After a fairy tale romance some couples awaken one day married to a stranger and ask themselves, "Who is this person I married?" Is it any wonder the divorce rate is so high today?

Room for growth in the relationship

Aspens are intriguing high altitude trees. In nature they co-exist with a distant cousin, the Colorado spruce, the state tree from which it's named. The two trees can grow together and co-exist in very tight quarters as they spread their branches and leaves to the sun and rain. However, there is competition as to which tree will find more nourishment over time, and each will outgrow the other depending upon the time of year.

The spruce tree, as an evergreen, remains visibly active in the winter. The aspen, however, loses its leaves and lies dormant throughout much of the winter awaiting a tremendous growth spurt during the spring and summer.

A union between two people is similar, as the rate of personal growth varies not only by gender but also by age and individual personality. At times, it may seem like one person may be trying to dominate the other, or at least gain more attention and personal growth. Only by communicating and having a strong healthy view of oneself can partners co-exist. Respect for each other is necessary for each to grow and thrive on their own timetables. It starts within. Find that loving self-awareness (know thyself), self-renewal (time to rejuvenate), and self-acceptance (love yourself) that we all possess.

Peeling the layers of the onion

So how do you get to the place where you feel safe with your partner in order to share weaknesses and shortcomings?

You should first ask yourself questions such as:

1. What personal areas of improvement do _I_ need to concentrate on and how can my partner help?
2. What areas of my past still bother _me_ today?
3. If I could change one thing about _myself_, what would that be?

Love is about seeing the darkest hour in someone and still being able to overlook and embrace those depths. Unconditional love requires the compassion to intuitively accept each other for who they are and to work through the difficulties.

Now the hard part comes as you ask each other:

4. What personal areas of improvement do _you_ think I need to concentrate on and how can _you_ help?
5. What areas of _our_ past still bother _you_ today?
6. If you could change one thing about _me_, what would that be?

Go slow through this process, respect and share your compassion for each other. A marriage counselor, therapist, or trusted friend may help. Making compromises and accepting a person for who they are, not who you want them to be, is key to happiness. This isn't a race and building a sincere connection that will survive takes time and patience.

#1—SPIRITUAL EXPLORATION:

The magic questions

No matter what a person's beliefs or religion, three questions remain unanswered:

Where did I come from?

What am I doing here?

Where am I going?

Religious and spiritual disciplines throughout the ages have been a means of trying to make sense of these questions. Self-confidence and self-worth are often tied to these answers. Three of the most controversial subjects people avoid discussing in searching for these answers are: sex, religion, and money. All the more reason dating couples should address these issues at an early juncture.

Who am I and who is this person I'm with?

Why have our life paths crossed?

Where have we been and where are we going?

Religion, spiritual experiences, and self-discovery may or may not help to answer these questions. But, it is the way a person goes about searching for the answers that can have a great impact on how they live with another in an intimate relationship.

For instance can a Catholic live happily with a Protestant? Can a Muslim live happily with a Jew? Under what religious education will the children be influenced and are there even going to be children? What possible pressures from families are the couples going to face regarding different religions?

The divisiveness of these issues can lead to divorce and unhappiness. Isn't it appropriate then to address them earlier rather than later?

Yoga, meditation, vision quests and more

Solo spiritual practices such as yoga, meditation, and vision quests are gaining in popularity. Usually they are more effective when done alone. Will each partner respect the other's right to privacy and solitude in order to practice these private spiritual experiences, allowing them the time and space to be who they really are? Jealousies or misunderstandings can develop regarding the solitude one spends without the other partner and this should be recognized early during spiritual evaluations (see last chapter Spacious Skies).

Let's define spirituality and religion remembering that each individual has their own personal experiences and interpretations. Spirituality is an individually based endeavor or mindset designed and customized by that person. Religions are rituals and practices, usually held in community, and designed by church leaders through the ages. Both spirituality and religion help to form a person's belief and value system.

Many singles search for a prospective partner in bars and during late night activities. This may seem like an easy way to meet new people spurred on by alcohol, which can help lessen shyness. However many churches, wellness and fitness centers, meditation communities, and yoga groups offer the same opportunities for singles to meet new partners on a more spiritual level. The quality of the initial introduction will probably be much clearer the next morning!

One man I know frequents Whole Foods to meet single women because he senses they will have a more health conscious attitude due to where and how they select their groceries. The environment in which you live can be helpful in finding those who will be more compatible for you to harmonize with.

#2—Intellectual Compatibility

Listen in at a cocktail party sometime and you will most likely hear a wide range of subjects and topics. Depending on the occasion and the audience, the discussions can range from the mundane weather and family matters to the more dynamic subjects of politics and economics. Where a person falls on the intellectual stimulation spectrum usually dictates the type of conversation they wish to have.

A marriage between an academic PhD and a high school drop out will look much different than one between couples who met in a college where they both obtained degrees. Not that one union is better than the other but both situations present their own unique challenges and differences.

Topics of conversations will likely differ from one couple to another but one thing about intimacy in a relationship is constant—it requires lots of conversation through the years.

#3—Hobbies and Outside Interests

It's amazing the number of people who get married and then go totally off on their own endeavors when it comes to personal time and interests. Having space to be you and get away from each other occasionally is important, having some common interests is even more vital. During the dating process, some couples spend an inordinate amount of time together with one person just pretending to like the main activities of the other. How else can you explain that soon after marriage the couple may no longer like the same activities?

It goes back to being up front and honest in the dating process. Let your partner know what you like and don't like to do. Also the circle of friends, that often has nearly doubled, will likely influence outside interests and hobbies.

Athletic activities help build the mind and body but engaging in cultural and intellectual activities shouldn't be overlooked.

#4—Do We Talk About SEX?

The Mars male ego treats the subject of sex in a number of different ways. Probably the most detrimental is that of conquest and domination. This gives Mars a false sense of short term self-worth and accomplishment while Venus is looking for the significance of a more long term connection.

In order to fulfill self-worth, most women are interested in their appearance and finding security while men are interested in power and reputation. Women want attention while men want respect, not that the two differ greatly. Women want to feel needed while men don't want to feel shamed. Of course, these traits can also apply to both sexes.

The sacred union of sex is more than a physical encounter. It is more than a good feeling or a good time. It is a unique opportunity for the universe to open at the same time for two human beings in something that continues to be indescribable, for how can you describe connecting to the universe?

With all sacred things, a certain respect is due a special relationship. Cheating on your girlfriend or your wife says something about your character. How can you be an honest man and of high integrity if you don't keep your word with the most important person in your life? It's like slapping God in the face. Your special partner was put on earth by God for _you_. Remember the sacredness of that event and the fact; if you are married, it's one of the Ten Commandments in the bible.

Compatibility as to frequency of sex can only be determined again through honest exchange between couples. NO ONE can predict how their sexual interests will develop over time, age and health. The good news for us guys—modern discoveries such as Viagra can help keep the spark in our fire.

Over time in truly enchanted relationships other binding forces become much more than just sex. Children, grandchildren, shared experiences, security of having each other in older age . . . these are what will become momentous as dating priorities expand into a strong connection of honesty that expands into a lifelong loving association.

Pray for help in finding your life partner

Some philosophies say there is a matching soul mate for every living soul. With the billions of people in the world, it makes sense there may be multiple soul mates for every living soul. So the search doesn't have to be the colloquial finding of the needle in the haystack.

Praying to a higher power for help to not only find but then recognize your life partner works for many. While some have been frustrated in personal prayer, I can provide personal testimony. After only two dates in high school and finding little enjoyment in socializing with Venus, I became discouraged and deflated. Rather than make another attempt, I prayed a simple prayer:

"God, when you find the right girl for me, please have her approach me instead of me having to do all the work."

This seemed like a simple request and one that would keep my fragile male ego intact. It also gave me an excuse not to interact with Venus for the time being.

Sure enough. In answer to prayers my Venus had a friend approach me on her behalf about asking her out. She is now my wife and we have been together for 38 years. The ironic thing about the situation is that the friend who approached me was my first date back before my prayer . . . and in a high school of nearly 500 students! God does have a sense of humor. So for all of the hype and advertising of Internet dating services, the simple power of prayer should not be overlooked.

The perfect partner: There isn't one

They say love is blind. Perhaps. But it isn't stupid. We've reviewed four priority areas of dating and the essence of honesty. Now it is time to try to evaluate what the perfect spouse would look like, knowing full well there is no such thing.

Being too rigid in your demands in looking for a partner is probably the biggest reason for so many single people out there today. In fact, some statistics show that, in the past 40 years, the percentage of people living alone has more than doubled from 13 percent to 28 percent.

The old adage that opposites attract may have some merit. Partners can offset extremes and compliment each other's weaknesses with their own strengths. Studies have shown that over time, people in close proximity have a tendency to gravitate toward each other's opposite extremes in views and lifestyles. Couples can make it over the imaginary "hump" and compromise some of their positions with each other and still feel good about themselves.

One acquaintance with perhaps too rigid a checklist calls them the 7cs. It is her way to remember what characteristics she is looking for in a man:

Conversation – Chemistry – Character – Christian

Confidence – Cultural – Comedy

A male friend counts having time to travel and her financial independence as two criteria he looks for in a partner.

Having a wish list may be a good idea. Just remember that it is a _wish_ list and to give the potential partner more than one chance—we all have bad days. Also, a discussion centered on your desired areas of personality and perceived traits is part of open and honest communications.

"You should respect each other and refrain from disputes; you should not, like water and oil, repel each other, but should, like milk and water, mingle together."

—Buddha

Chapter Two

All systems go: Healthy marriage attitudes; they can change over time

I was always shy around girls. At least I thought I was. Perhaps it was my lack of confidence, always thinking I did not have anything worthwhile to say, or that my poor eyesight and bothersome contact lenses didn't allow me to always recognize classmates in order to greet them properly. I felt self-conscious and that was the barrier that kept me tied up inside.

Within, it may have been my father's subservient relationship with his mother (my grandmother) and his corresponding treatment of my mother that added to my uncertainty regarding women. My grandmother always seemed to browbeat my father and then he would take it out on my mother. At an early age, I once attempted to stand up for my mother and wound up taking the full force of rage from my grandmother. That experience made it difficult for me to stand up for my mother, wife, and family in later years. I shied away from several important confrontations on their behalf. I just didn't have many examples of men in my life that projected how to interact with women.

I am not unusual for my generation of men, who were taught not to cry, to disconnect from my emotions, and to always show strength. So I was unsure what "love" really meant. Macho aggression required that I ignore the emotional whims of the fairer sex.

But some of that changed during my senior year of high school when an adorable co-ed, who later became my wife, started showing an interest in me. With nowhere to run, I discovered the wonders of dating, sharing my life with another person and, of course, sex.

It was during this period I thought I could have almost anything I wanted if I worked hard and outsmarted everyone. Back then, it didn't matter if this wonderful girl went away. I thought I would just find another.

Through the first ten years of my marriage, that was basically the attitude I lived with. I thought, if she doesn't like it, she knows where to find the door and she can hit the highway. I subscribed to the concept of marriage as a contract rather than a covenant. In a contract, I _take_ my wife as mine whereas in a covenant, I _give myself_ to my wife.

Although having children began to temper me somewhat, I was still used to getting my own way because, as the oldest son, it had been ingrained in my psyche since childhood that I deserved certain privileges. I had been raised in a strong male family structure and I was rarely willing to yield my perceived status as "head of the household."

Caring for my two children awakened me to the insensitivity that shrouded my marriage. The realization dawned on me that this woman might really be my soul mate and it introduced me to a new spiritual concept of love. Still, the idea of her ever leaving me seemed remote. It was part of the armor I put on everyday going into the business battlefield. I couldn't fail. I couldn't lose. I had to be one of the best. Anything else was showing weakness.

Mid-life crisis is as mysterious as it is painful. It is one of those experiences you are glad you had but wouldn't want to do again. Unfortunately, for many, mid-life crisis can become post mid-life crisis can become old-age crisis. I was heading in that direction.

However, it was during a men's weekend retreat of *The Mankind Project* that the light really went off for me. I was bunking next to Jim, a total stranger, who was facing divorce. Jim told me his story of marrying a woman who won the title of Ms. Minnesota. He then started taking her for granted. He said he even showed her off as a trophy to his friends and then left her at home while he went out with the guys in the evenings.

At this point in Jim's remorse, he was attending the weekend in an attempt to salvage what he could of his marriage. Jim courted Ms. Minnesota for only a few months before marrying her, but now he was courting her full time simply to stay married.

The saddest part of the story, he told me, was coming home one evening and finding his bags packed at the door. She told him to get out and never come back.

Jim's impending divorce wasn't what put the fear into me. It was Jim's statement that he never saw it coming. Logic would say the opposite; Jim should have clearly seen his wife was unhappy. But the obvious often goes unnoticed in self-denial. I also knew self-denial and it had visited me all too often. For years, I had been involved in guy stories regarding dominance and control at home.

I looked around during the men's retreat. I was not the best looking; not the smartest; not the wealthiest. It occurred to me; divorce knows no boundaries. Jim's fate could easily happen to me at any moment. For when I was done looking around at the group of men, I was still just me.

Going forward, I reviewed my life and made a commitment to change my marriage attitude. However, as it frequently does in life, I found my internal pendulum had swung too far to the other extreme. I was now absorbed in guilt and shame about my past treatment of my wife.

Although my marriage looked much different now, I found it unhealthy for another reason. Instead of letting go of the past and forgiving myself for unacceptable behavior, I was trying too hard to please my wife.

I soon lost the essence of being myself; of being who I really was. My self-confidence waned and I lived in fear of divorce.

Past comments from friends such as; my wife "must be a saint" or "my wife deserves a medal" started to have an impact on me. People become saints after suffering, sacrifice, and overcoming major adversity. Was I the devil? People receive medals for heroic action. Was it heroic to live with me? Were my friends complimenting my wife, insulting me, or both?

It took a period of time before I finally came back to a balanced center and put things in perspective. Now I don't give weight to comments of others who know nothing of our relationship but instead, I evaluate my behavior with my wife directly. I communicate how I really feel and what

I believe. I no longer fear divorce and have quit berating myself when I make mistakes. I forgive myself and so does my wife.

Going back to the weekend where I first met Jim, I can't say for sure if learning about Jim's desperate situation saved my marriage. These are some of life's questions that remain unanswered. What I do know is I never looked at my wife the same way again. My appreciation of her is blossoming, and so is our love.

I finally understand my wife's saying:

"I love you more today than yesterday but not as much as tomorrow."

"In this same way husbands ought to love their wives as their own bodies. He who loves his wife loves himself."

—Ephesians 5:28

Chapter Three

Come in mission control: What do you ask for . . . money, power, sex, bliss?

When King Solomon was asked the same question, he told the Lord he wished for wisdom to understand himself and others. Because his request had been unselfish and he had not asked for material things of the world, he was granted the gift of wisdom.

Whether in a friendship, a business association, solving a problem, or just happy everyday life, I've gotten a little greedier asking for more than just wisdom. Here is what I ask and pray for:

Courage + Strength + Wisdom + Humility + Patience

= COMPASSSION

These are the character traits I seek, often using meditation to find them. If the five characteristics above are combined, I've discovered the ultimate trait in dealing with others = compassion.

COURAGE

You've been there before; when courage has fled like the wind. Remember that action not taken; that word or two of encouragement not given to someone; the question not asked; not getting involved or turning the other way?

How often do we ask for the courage to make things right in our relationships? Courage to forgive and to ask for forgiveness. Courage to ask what we can do to make things right, go to counseling; to do whatever it takes.

Self-awareness often requires courage so we can grow personally. It takes looking at ourselves from a third party perspective to detect our weaknesses and faults. Sometimes called shadows, these are the flawed parts of us we try to hide, suppress, or deny. But shadows can also become our gold or strengths when we have the courage to stand up and recognize them within ourselves.

For instance, aggressiveness can be a drawback. It can alienate people, cause friction, ruin friendships, and lose business opportunities. But when tempered, aggressiveness can also create new associations and friends through courageous introductions, win new business contracts, and smooth over problems with bold mediation and compromise. Courage can unlock your weaknesses and shadows so you can modify or change them.

There are any number of reasons we don't follow our courage to act on our intuition and instincts—whatever you want to call those messages sent from God or a higher spirit—but in the end it comes down to a four letter word . . . Fear.

Any good therapist can tell you overcoming fear can take a number of personal commitments, changing habits and rituals, personal analysis, remolding belief systems, lifestyle changes, and the list goes on. But no matter which direction you take it requires . . .

STRENGTH

A classic story of strength comes from the bible's Samson and Delilah. Samson's massive physical strength, as the story goes, allowed him to kill more than 1,000 Philistine soldiers in a single day swinging nothing more than the jawbone of a mule.

But even more powerful than outer strength is that which flows from within. We find that inner strength finally failed Sampson when he confided in Delilah. He granted her what she was after—the secret of his physical strength was related to the length of his hair. Apparently their prior dating experience had been less than honest.

Delilah betrays Sampson, one of the Old Testament's worst betrayals, and tells his secret to the Philistines. His hair was shaved while he slept. Then his eyes were gouged out and he was bound to slavery. Others now commanded him and harnessed his physical strength once his hair had grown back.

Even blinded, humiliated, and bound by chains, Sampson still was master of his inner strength. He used it nobly in the end by crumbling the pillars, caving the temple, and killing his tormentors along with himself.

How often do you pray for inner strength, both personally and as a couple, to make it through another day? Strength to awaken in a positive mood, show affection to each other, go to work to provide for your family, get up in the middle of the night with a young one? Strength to overcome the obstacles we all face and to carry the crosses we all bear?

A strong mind and discipline can help us find and hold on to inner . . .

WISDOM

Intuition, instinct, indigenous wisdom of our ancestors. We all possess this inner wisdom but don't always listen to it. Your wife or significant other may have said something like this in the past, *"you didn't listen to me but when someone else says it, why do you believe it?"*

I've been there and it took me many years to digest the comment, but in the end my wife was right. To finally make sense out of all of this and answer her question, I walked over and touched the end of her nose. She looked at me somewhat perturbed. *"Can you see the spot I just touched on the end of your nose?"* I taunted her.

And that is exactly why inner wisdom can be such an elusive animal. We all have it. It's available to us at any time and as accessible as touching our own nose. We can sense it but we can't see it or hear it because it is so close to us.

When was the last time you stayed quiet, meditated, and listened to what direction you should take in a crisis? To ask and pray that your actions will be wise ones, not harmful to yourself or to others? To listen to the steps that need to be taken in dealing with others or to seek out a mentor offering wisdom before taking action?

Relational wisdom includes attempting to indentify those actions and comments that trigger irritation in the other partner. Triggers are something we do or don't do that annoys another. These are the irritations that often simmer unchallenged over time. The reactions to these triggers then come out sideways instead of in a direct and open discussion. Communicating on _what_ action specifically triggers someone, _why_ it triggers them, and a request that the other person _discontinue_ that behavior can settle many conflicts.

A word of caution. In the rare case where these triggers are an important part of who you are, and they still bother the other person, then more discussion is required. You need to continue to be who you are.

Jointly making a list of each person's triggers will help raise awareness. For instance loud music before dinner irritated me so I was able to buy my wife great lightweight stereo headphones. My wife likes social drinking so I've acquired a taste for "mocktails,"—imitations of drinks without the alcohol.

Just listen to the wisdom that comes from your heart, as well as your mind. We all know inherently the right path to take. Slow down. Access that inner wisdom that whispers to you. It will guide you to the level of the person you want to be.

Don't isolate yourself. Find support groups, mentors, friends, or a knowledgeable therapist. They can help you listen to your inner voices of wisdom by asking the right questions. A worldwide program for men that is worth looking into that has more than 25 years experience: www. mankindproject.org.

In furthering personal wisdom, my landmine theory requires that you think ahead about a situation before you step into it and blow yourself up. Be prepared to make a PROACTIVE decision rather than a REACTIVE decision by contemplating possible scenarios before they occur.

Temptations will always be coming your way. What will you do if solicited by another woman? What will happen if someone offers you an illegal bribe? Being PROACTIVE means preparing yourself regarding what action you will take before these hypotheticals occur.

God grant me the serenity
to accept the things I cannot change;
<u>courage</u> to change the things I can;
and <u>wisdom</u> to know the difference.
-Reinhold Niebuhr

Immersing oneself in wisdom carries with it probably one of the most difficult character traits to achieve . . .

HUMILTY

Why is humility so hard for most of us?

Perhaps it has something to do with Mr. Ego, the voice that thinks it protects us, gains us respect from others, and tells us who we really are. Don't believe him. He's not of the real world but the one we fabricate to protect us from FEAR. Have we made it around the circle yet from the discussion of courage? Fear does show up when we least expect it and our ego tries to keep that from happening.

Contrary to what some might think, it takes tremendous courage, along with strength and wisdom, to be humble.

The Bible states . . .
Blessed are the meek for they shall inherit the earth.
—Matthew 5:5

Some identify humility with weakness and the meek—nothing could be further from the truth.

We are usually at our finest moment when basking in the light of humility. It allows us to better see ourselves and the world around us. It puts others at ease—they like us better—because they know we see ourselves as only part of the picture and not the whole picture.

Asking for humility is not asking for weakness. Some of the greatest sages and leaders throughout history have carried tremendous humility at their side . . . Gandhi, Mother Teresa, Nelson Mandela, Martin Luther King, and Jesus.

So why is it easier for them to display humility than us? Perhaps that comes from something called . . .

PATIENCE

"Hurry up so we can get there . . ."

My mother used that comment sarcastically during family vacations. It wasn't until years later I understood the meaning of her comment. If we didn't slow down and take our time, we were going to miss some of the best parts of the trip.

Enlightened ones will tell you it's the journey, not the destination, that highlights the path we are on. It's the journey that we will hold on to long after other memories have faded. Try and explain that to a corporate executive who busily churns the data from which he will make his afternoon presentation.

Is patience something we are born with or is it a technique to be mastered; a discipline of recurring awareness and constant practice?

The new born infants I observed, my two fine sons, came screaming into the world wanting something and in a hurry to get it. So while some may have greater aptitudes toward exhibiting patience, it appears to be a trait that needs to be practiced and acquired.

How often do we ask and pray for patience during an ordeal or conflict rather than obsessing and/or rushing headlong into a situation we will later regret?

My grandfather was not one for patience. While he accomplished great things in his life including having Congress name a lake after him, he may have alienated as many people as he gathered who admired him.

On my grandfather's desk sat the saying:

On the plains of hesitation bleach bones of unnumbered thousands who at the dawn of victory sat down to wait and waiting died.

My father, who was responsible for daily newspaper editorials most of his life, had another anecdote:

Always wait 24 hours or longer before writing any editorial that might be slanted with personal emotions rather than facts.

The point of this discussion is that, in everything, patience requires balance. On the one hand, don't let procrastination disguise itself as patience in your home. On the other, however, displaying patience is probably the cornerstone on which to lay courage, strength, wisdom, and humility. Accomplishing this foundation brings us . . .

COMPASSION

How do you define compassion?

Is it merely throwing a homeless person a couple dollars or does it include being able to look into and through the eyes of the homeless person, tasting the world they live in?

Having the _courage_ to stand up for someone who needs help, the _strength_ to carry on—even though you may be tired and worn out—when another needs your help, the _wisdom_ to say and do the right things, the _humility_ to step aside and give credit to someone else, or the _patience_ to just sit and listen. If you can do these things when those around you have no awareness, then you have achieved one of the most cherished aspects of love . . . _compassion_.

Giving back. Helping others. This is truly the best medicine one can receive for healing themselves. When we help others, we help ourselves.

As a species, we are all part of the walking wounded in this world. It depends on how we have let our individual traumas impact us and, more importantly, what we have done to heal ourselves.

Showing compassion for ourselves, however, must happen first before we can have it for others. As one version of the Golden Rule (see chapter 6) states: **Love your neighbor as yourself.** So my version of the Golden Rule includes first reviewing whether you love yourself. Then you can more fully love your neighbor.

Here is a quick check on how much you love yourself:

-How often do you spend time by yourself just to relax and rest?

-Do you give yourself more personal pep talks or do you more often berate yourself?

-How often do you congratulate yourself?

-Do you take special trips and vacation time to celebrate major accomplishments?

-How often do you body and suntan lotion?

-Do you schedule regular body massages?

It's like the flight attendants' instructions before takeoff. In a crisis, passengers should put on their own oxygen masks before they help others. If you can't take care of and love yourself, how are you ever going to show real compassion and care for another?

So in closing, I will ask and pray for:

Courage to write today.

Strength to continue writing.

Wisdom to write that which will be beneficial to myself and others.

Humility to realize I'm not a great writer, and I don't have to be.

Patience to overcome the voices of doubts and setbacks in my writing.

Compassion while writing so I don't beat myself up with my own expectations and that what I write will help myself and others.

"Men are respectable only as they respect"
—Ralph Waldo Emerson

Chapter Four

Straight and level flight: Balancing happiness

Balancing time can be a major factor in leading a happy life.

Here are four simple areas to review in your life that were presented during a Wall Street financial stress management course and can probably help you avoid stress, anxiety, and depression:

1. **Exercise**
2. **Work**
3. **Social**
4. **Solitude**

These areas are not listed in any particular order. Also, time allocation is not necessarily meant to be divided equally. In fact, each individual personality and age will dictate the comfortable amount of time spent in balancing your ongoing life experience.

Regular introspection should indicate those areas you are overextended in and those areas you need to spend more time on. For instance, your soul may cry out for solitude if you've just spent every night for a week at dinner parties and social events. Exercise and sports may be calling to you after you have worked an 80-hour week without any physical activity.

Finding quality time to spend with those you love is what life is all about. No matter what your accomplishments; a healthy marriage and/or raising compassionate ethical children should be the legacy you want to leave behind.

Time is the one common gift granted to us all from birth to death. It is something no one can take from us.

You may say such things as imprisonment or being forced to attend a business event are attempts at stealing time. Not true. No matter where you are or whatever circumstance you find yourself in, the time for your body and mind to function continues on. You might not be spending time the way you wish, but you are being allocated time every second, minute, hour, week, month and year. Don't let the clock tick away while you are unaware of this gift in your life.

Exercise

Aligning your mind, body and spirit may have become an overused cliché but focusing on regular physical and mental exercise is not. Most medical experts tell us it's an ingredient to a healthy and long life. The amount of time spent in physical activity is often not important, but rather the frequency and consistency of exercise. As we age we should be spending more time on exercise, nutrition, medication when necessary, and medical consultations. Having problems sleeping at night? Depressed? Anxiety-ridden? Feeling sluggish both mentally and physically?

Scientists tell us such things as serotonin, chemicals in the brain, help to keep a person happier throughout the day and night. Athletes know this from their regular practice and performance. Many discover their superior talents and excel in sports due to this natural "high" they get through releasing these brain chemicals during physical activity.

And don't forget mental exercise. It has been proven that the effects of Alzheimer's disease are held off longer for those who actively engage their minds and who have attained a higher level of education. Activities requiring expanded use of the mind such as checkers, chess, reading, crossword puzzles, writing, participating in art and music are worthwhile. Memory exercises are also available via computer and the Internet. Fitness centers help people maintain muscle tone and build stamina; mental gymnastics can help tone memory, enhance clear thinking, and enhance imagination.

Don't forget how you fuel those exercises. A nutritionist can help you spot dietary concerns, such as too much sugar, which can create problems both mentally and physically. It may sound corny but mothers and grandmothers told us when we were younger to let our stomach digest before continuing physical activities (they care about us on Venus). Resting after meals is what the Mexican siesta is all about. Eat smaller portions. Watch the labels on the food packages before you buy them. You really are what you put in your mouth.

In physical activity, as with other things in life, take it slow and don't push yourself too hard. And don't forget the first part of the Golden Rule—love yourself.

Self-acceptance

Don't let your own or other's expectations rule your life

Take a look at your mistakes and then LET THEM GO

Review your successes and be gentle with yourself when you fail

Work

God, a higher power, the universe . . . these forces use a variety of ways to get you to connect to others. Whether driven by greed, the need to keep your family financially secure, or a more pure motivation of simply being in service to others; our business endeavors serve the very simple process of connecting us to each other.

I chose the name Aspen Grove Capital Management for my business for one reason. It best exemplifies the interconnection of all things. An aspen grove is the largest living organism in the world since its roots are interconnected under ground and thus invisible to us. Instead of producing cones or seeds, it simply sprouts a new offshoot.

There is one grove in Utah that spans over 100 hundred acres and is one plant. If one tree becomes ill or needs nourishment, the surrounding trees can come to the rescue through the invisible connected root system. Our connection to each other is likewise invisible. We have our own support system of spouse, family, friends, therapists, religious leaders, and others who come to our rescue when we are down.

Perhaps one of the most destructive and invisible addictions in society today is that of the workaholic. Divorces and broken families are left in the wake of this rarely discussed addiction.

Getting ahead, providing for the family, self-satisfaction, and ego. These are all reasons to justify long hours and sacrifices away from home in the name of our business interests. Like anything in life, a balance is necessary to be successful in the arena that really counts—your spouse and family.

The next time you are considering putting in extra hours during evenings or on weekends, check and see if it is in alignment with the four areas of balance: work, exercise, solitude and social. It's doubtful you will regret you didn't work longer hours when you are on your death bed.

Social

Most people are wired to be creatures of social interaction, some more than others. Family life becomes the initial social interaction as we nurture and teach our young ones how to function in a social setting. Parents model activity through their actions with others, whether in a personal or business environment.

Anti-social behavior, such as social anxiety, creates stress in many people and should not be looked upon as some kind of personality defect. This is where the balance between social and solitude is so important. We all need to spend enough time alone in self-renewal storing up self-confidence and recharging our energy to survive in an active social setting.

Self-renewal

Don't take on mistakes of the past. Ask others not to remind you of them.

Take regular breaks during the day. A noon nap might help recharge you.

Keep a file of written compliments from others, achievements, and volunteer work. Review this material regularly.

Make a list of the talents you have and how they are often used for others.

Another anecdote from my grandfather that was passed down to me through my father:

Choose your friends, don't let them choose you.

If you want to play tennis and improve, find a competitor who is better than you. In associations with others, finding someone with greater insight will help you improve your own.

There is either a draining or filling up of personal energy when we interact with others. In a good balanced friendship the ebb and flow of giving and taking should balance out over time. But we all have had experiences with those "energy vampires" that seem to suck every last bit of energy we have when we are with them.

That's not to say we shouldn't have situations with others where we are trying to support, listen to, and offer to mentor them if that will help. SELF-AWARENESS is the key. We need to be aware if it is a draining friendship and how much of our energy we are willing to give to it. When we are giving all of our time and energy to others, and not receiving renewal energy in return, then our own world can suffer.

Self-awareness

Meditate and review the past day to see where there were areas of conflict and how best to resolve them.

Pray before the day begins for happiness for yourself and others.

Anticipate potential conflicts so you can be proactive rather than reactive.

Connect and associate with those who energize you and fill you with positive energy rather than drain you and give off negativity.

Solitude

One sign of spiritual maturity is the ability to spend time alone and enjoy it. When I first attempted solo camping trips or isolating myself in my writing, I became very uncomfortable. Confronting one's demons in the middle of the night, isolated for miles from another human being, can be a daunting task.

Solitude is like a commodity that we take within and store in our psyche. However, as we store solitude, time and space can become our enemies. Managing time efficiently includes where you are during the day and night and who you are with. However, planning ahead can create anxiety and take over the thought process. The ability to rest the mind from the pressures and distractions of time and space allows restoration of the soul.

How many of us have sat through meetings and conversations with others, not giving our undivided attention? We are thinking about where we should be or who we would rather be with instead of what is happening right now in the present.

Sometimes we just have to put up a stop sign and bring things to a standstill in our lives. It's like the title of the Broadway musical; *Stop the World—I Want to Get Off*. Getting quality self-renewal requires personal time and space without anyone else being present or interrupting. Some people even schedule time on their calendars on a regular basis just to be alone. Have a regular time each day to spend in meditation to discover the difference it can make.

We all need to find our own personal routines and rituals that will renew our souls and keep our inner compass on course. Hopefully balancing these four areas of your life will work for you—it has for me these past two decades.

One last note to yourself—Annual life plan

A life plan differs from a business plan in that it addresses you as a person. It's not about making money, sales and marketing goals or winning new customers. It's about addressing your own goals, weaknesses, relationships, and strengths.

One way to go about it is to classify priorities into the Five Fs—Faith, Family, Friends, Fitness and Finance. It's also good to include a bucket list; those things you dream about and hope to accomplish someday.

It's an opportunity to plan time with family and friends, set routines and good habits, address bad habits and things you want to modify in your life. A good plan should include physical workouts and sports activities as well as mental challenges, self-improvement, reading, or educational classes.

Using daily routines can establish more consistency. I use acronyms to help remember them. One example is my morning routine **MLEEPOW**:

Medication—if needed and vitamins
Lotion—to avoid skin cancer
Eat—healthy and fresh foods
Exercise—frequency, not endurance
Pray/meditate—for peace of mind
Organize (I also do this the night before)
Write—the hard part

Thoughts lead to actions that become habits, which define character that leads us to destiny.—Anthony Robbins.

Here is an example of my 2012 life plan:

Life Plan—2012 "Year of Methodical discipline"

Live the life the creator intended you to live

Mission: Inspire and encourage at least one person everyday

Routine—   <u>Daily</u>   <u>Nightly</u>
                     Meds   Tomorrow plan out
                     Lotion   Activity for tonight
                     Eat   Lotion
                     Exercise   Prayer/meditate
                     Prayer/meditate
                     Organize
                     Write

Balance—exercise, solitude, work, social

1. Work—   *Read ½ hour daily Write daily*
                     Tuesday talks on reading
                     Available
                     Dependable
                     Adaptable

2. Family—   *Dad—spend more time visiting*
                     Sons—hunting/fishing time
                     Wife—tennis/dinner/golf
                     Brother, sister—call regularly

3. *Eliminations/empowerment*
>   *Limited hobbies*
>   *Use maintenance man*
>   *Obsession—use positive rituals*
>   *Lower priorities down list*

4. *Faith—*
>   *Yoga, sweat lodge, church*
>   *Men's group activities*
>   *Self-renewal*
>   *Self-awareness*
>   *Self-acceptance*

5. *Finance—*
>   *Review credit cards*
>   *Check investments monthly*
>   *Change investments quarterly*

6. *Fitness—*
>   *Exercise arms/legs*
>   *Biking*

Trek Himalayas

7. *Bucket List—*

>   *Deal blackjack professionally Colorado elk hunt*
>   *Salmon fishing in Alaska*

8. *Friends—*   *Tennis, bocce ball, dinners*

Like life, the possibilities of your connection with yourself, wife, friends, and others are endless when you approach them with enthusiasm and creativity.

"The first duty of love is to listen."
—**Paul Tillich**

Chapter Five

Meteor showers ahead: Embracing obsession
Rid yourself of negative thoughts

Obsession is almost always associated with unwanted feelings or emotions that cause mental distress. If it involves our security or safety, then fear can also create anxiety. Unchecked jealousy, anger, and sadness can fester and deteriorate even the healthiest of relationships.

The Five Steps to resolve obsession—those revolving echoes you hear in your own mind over and over—can bring a calming peace by silencing unwanted thoughts and inner voices:

1. **Awareness**
2. **Introspection**
3. **Expressing emotions—journaling**
4. **Prayer—asking questions**
5. **Meditation—listening**

Being negative and complaining around your significant other is the easiest way to ruin the day or evening. Obsession can lead to losing your temper and snapping at that dearest and most supportive person in your life.

Men have been struggling with obsession since primitive times with worries about the elements of survival . . . where the next meal would come from and providing security for their families. Obsession generates anxiety and anxiety can create fear related anger, which makes us strike out against others.

Obsession often feeds and embraces what some term "monkey mind" because of the crazy chatter that forms in the thought stream. It's like trying not to think of the proverbial pink elephant. The more you try not to think of it, the more it persists.

I'm a champion obsessor. It's something I have an aptitude for and it comes naturally. Even though it requires little practice, I have spent many hours embracing the detrimental process of obsession.

Hopefully this simple five step process, _awareness_, _introspection_, _journaling_, _prayer_, and _meditation_, may be of benefit in releasing those inner demons that stalk you. It requires quiet time alone to listen to your inner wisdom, that which comes from God or whatever you consider your higher power.

I ask questions in prayer, listen in meditation, and let my frustrations out through pen and paper. For those who prefer verbal rather than written form, a tape recorder would also suffice for clarifying and releasing frustrations. Release anger by letting it flow through your pen or recorder. Remember, you can keep it private and no one has to read or listen to your anger. It will end up being a healthier way to vent your frustrations.

I have had to repeat this Five Step process several times on the same subject in the past; usually after some time has passed. Don't get discouraged it if doesn't work the first time through; just keep trying.

Here is an example of using the system after something that might be said between a couple. A wife has called her husband overweight, she did it in front of others, and it has been bothering him all evening. Here are the five steps to overcoming obsession following the thought patterns that might develop after the man sits quietly alone and concentrates on the questions below:

1. What is the lesson God is offering him?

No one is kind 100 percent of the time including his wife. He needs to be patient with others when they are unkind and don't offer the praise and support he seeks. Perhaps he needs to look at his health and how he is taking care of himself, since his body should be the most sacred thing in his possession. He has been given gifts that need to be cherished if he is to be happy and help others—his body being one of those gifts.

His insecurities about his wife leaving him and finding someone else come to the surface when she talks this way.

2. What can he see in himself about his wife's behavior?

He has told her she is overweight in the past. He has even said such things about her family and friends. There are a couple of reasons he has done this.

Probably foremost is his ego and desire to have a wife others will envy. He wants their respect and if they see he's attracted and married a fit and good looking lady, they will think more highly of him.

Of course these thoughts are egotistical judgments he wants to discontinue. It's time for him to address them so they go away.

Secondly, he worries that being overweight can lead to health problems and even death. He does not want health problems himself nor does he want them for his wife. Fear of death and health has entered into his thinking.

3. **A personal journal entry, whether he shares it with his wife or not, helps to clarify and release the emotions he feels about what has happened.**

Dear Joy,

You said I was overweight and I resent that. You are indeed as much overweight as I am, if not more. Talk about calling the kettle black. What a BITCH! (Remember, this letter doesn't have to be shared with anyone).

The fact that you did it in front of our friends only magnifies the situation. It was a chicken shit and hurtful thing to do.

I'm not sure why you did this. Maybe you were mad at me about something else that happened with the kids or an incident at home earlier in the week.

No matter why you did it, it hurt my feelings and showed disrespect in front of others. I was embarrassed and continue to obsess over it. I want to quit thinking about it and flush it out of my mind.

I hope you realize the insensitivity of your actions and take steps to eliminate such idiotic behavior in the future.

4. **Pray for help in his marriage and to take those thoughts away that are bothering him so he can have peace from within.**

Dear God,

Please help me in my marriage. We seem to have problems on a regular basis and I need your help in order to be happy and not end up in divorce. We all need help but are often afraid to ask for it. I'm asking for it right now.

I can't seem to quit thinking about what she did. I'm embarrassed and angry. Please take these things from me so I can focus my attention on my family and on helping others.

Help me to forgive and forget. _Please tell me God what steps I need to take to stop this obsession._

Amen

5. **Meditate on what he has to do to stop the obsessing.**

Prayer is when we are talking. Meditation is when we listen. Some of the best insights, whether through creativity, imagination, or just plain common sense, come to us when we use solitude. Just go off alone, quiet the mind, and let ideas flow from the subconscious. This is best done if you allow your mind to go blank and concentrate on your breathing as you meditate. Closing your eyes or focusing on something like a candle can help keep unwanted thoughts away. When they come, and they constantly do, just let them pass on by like a raft in a river. If you reach out and grab that raft of thoughts, then they will continue to distract your meditation.

The steps needed to stop obsessing in this case were for him to talk to his wife about it further so she knows he is upset, letting go of his egotistical thoughts that keep him embarrassed and feeling disrespected, and forgiveness for her unkind comment.

"Forgiveness means it finally becomes unimportant that you hit back."
—**Anne Lamont**

"To err is human, to forgive, divine."
—**Alexander Pope**

"As I walked out the door toward the gate that would lead to my freedom, I knew if I didn't leave my bitterness and hatred behind, I'd still be in prison."
—**Nelson Mandela**

Now let's take this method a step further and apply it to a business situation. Let's use an example of a former friend who owes money and has refused to pay. So the thinking process goes like this:

1. What is the lesson God is offering me?

I cannot CONTROL everything in my life. Life is not fair and I have to downgrade my EXPECTATIONS of others. I do get unexpected positive breaks in my life just as I get negative ones and they mostly balance out over time. Why don't I recall the unexpected positive breaks I get in life as much as the bad breaks?

I've gotten unexpected bills discounted, favors from others, and a job promotion out of nowhere. I tend to forget and not fully appreciated the unexpected good things that happen to me.

Don't MAGNIFY the negative. I don't really need the money that is owed me and it won't change my lifestyle so I should be happy and GRATEFUL for what I do have (sometimes listing out blessings in your life is helpful).

Finally another lesson here is not letting your EGO run overtime. Issues such as betrayal, abandonment, and disrespect feed the obsession monster. Recognizing them and then releasing that energy into the universe is the challenge.

2. Owning my actions and taking responsibility

I was the one who made the decision to enter into a business agreement with this person so I shouldn't put the full blame on him. I have broken agreements with others both consciously and unconsciously in the past.

There is a blessing of self-awareness in seeing my own shadow or weakness in another person. In the past I have taken things from others and given nothing in return. By having this happen to me I can hopefully avoid doing it again to others.

3. Journaling/releasing the anger

Dear Former Friend,

You are an egotistical bastard who has ruined our friendship by refusing to pay me what was due. You made money off my clients, pocketed the money and used it for frivolous luxuries like second and third homes, jets, and prestigious materialistic endeavors. I think you are trying to show me you are superior by attempting to outsmart me in our business dealings.

You know deep down you are wrong. Hopefully someday you will make amends and act honorably in your dealings with me and others. The fact you have paid some money to me in the past is encouraging and in my opinion indicates you really want to do the right thing. Now if you will just make the effort and pay me everything you owe me.

I'm writing you this letter to feel better and flush out my frustrations and anger. I probably won't send it but know that the energy I'm releasing can be felt and is helpful to me.

I pray for the others in your life who you have hurt in this manner, as well as those whom I also have hurt. I pray that God might soften your heart, your ego, and your sensitivity toward others.

Signed,

Hurt and frustrated

Now if you examine the letter, it releases a tinge of anger in the opening. In the latter years of my life it seems I don't have to get as mad to release my feelings. You may differ and, if so, this is the time and place to let it all hang out. Remember, no one has to see your private letters.

Also, you should not try to reason and rationalize in your mind but let the feelings come out from your heart. Instead of holding it in, you might have just told this person how much he hurt you and how disappointed you were.

The irony of this is; if you continue to give further time and energy to the situation in your thoughts, on top of the money he owes you, you create undue stress and anxiety along the way. In order to maintain your power, you need to stop the obsession.

The more honesty and the more trash you throw out in your writing, the better you will feel and the sooner you will release the obsession that is holding you hostage.

4. Praying: so I can be happy and help others.

God,

I need help with this one. It is taking time and energy from me so I can't help others and myself. I know you put me in this world to be happy and cheerful. I can't do that as long as these inner demons remind me of this situation.

I am angry at this person and feel hurt. He is wrong. Please take this burden from me so I might be of better service to you, others, and myself. Tell me what steps *I* need to take so I can quit obsessing and move on.

5. Meditating/listening to the steps I need to take.

The steps that come during meditation . . .

A. I have already told him in an email what my position is on the matter. Talk to him personally about how it has impacted me.
B. Compare what others have done to me in the past so I realize this isn't the first time I have been disappointed and also realize it won't be the last.
C. Put final closure on the subject by telling myself I won't get paid and the money won't make a difference in how I live my life anyway.
D. FORGIVE him.

Forgiveness can be very hard for most and impossible for a few. Be among the strong of mind and heart by being able to forgive.

"The weak can never forgive. Forgiveness is the attribute of the strong."
—**Mahatma Gandhi**

"Forgiveness is not an occasional act, it is a constant attitude."
—**Martin Luther King Jr.**

"Resentment is like drinking poison and then hoping it will kill your enemies."
—**Nelson Mandela**

"To be wronged is nothing, unless you continue to remember it."
—**Confucius**

If you don't find peace of mind in the Five Step process the first few times, don't give up! It takes practice, discipline, and consistency to overcome obsession.

"If we lose love and self-respect for each other, this is how we finally die."

—Maya Angelou

Chapter Six

Truth in the universe: The Golden Rule

Common theme in religions and disciplines

Forgiveness comes in many shapes and colors. However, it can be one of the hardest acts to accomplish, especially when you have been deeply wounded by another.

When reviewing the many expressions of the Golden Rule, I find forgiveness of oneself is the first step in how we treat others.

One common thread runs throughout most religions and spiritual practices. It is the foundation on which all relationships flourish. Its essence is about compassion and empathy for others and it is expressed many different ways.

But before you can practice what many call the Golden Rule, it requires loving and connecting to yourself first. For how can you fully care about and show compassion to another while carrying contempt, shame, and guilt toward yourself?

Ancient Egyptian
"Do for one who may do for you, that you may cause him thus to do."
—Tale of the Eloquent Peasant

Ancient Greece
"May I do to others as I would that they should do unto me."
—Plato, 4th Century

"Do not do to others that which would anger you if others did it to you."
—Socrates, 5th Century

Bahá'í:
"Ascribe not to any soul that which thou wouldst not have ascribed to thee, and say not that which thou doest not."
"Blessed is he who preferreth his brother before himself."
—Baha'u'llah

Brahmanism:
"This is the sum of Dharma [duty]: Do naught unto others which would cause you pain if done to you."
—Mahabharata, 5:1517

Buddhism:
"A state that is not pleasing or delightful to me, how could I inflict that upon another?"
—Samyutta Nikaya v. 353

Christianity:
"You shall love your neighbor as yourself."
—Matthew 22:39

Confucianism:
"One should not behave towards others in a way which is disagreeable to oneself."
—Mencius VII.A.4

Hinduism:
"This is the sum of duty: do naught unto others which would cause you pain if done to you."
—Mahabharata 5:1517

Islam:
"No one of you is a believer until he desires for his brother that which he desires for himself."
—Hadith of an-Nawawi 13

Jainism:
"A man should wander about treating all creatures as he himself would be treated."
—Sutrakritanga 1.11.33

Judaism:
". . . thou shalt love thy neighbor as thyself."
—Leviticus 19:18

Native American Spirituality:
"All things are our relatives; what we do to everything, we do to ourselves. All is really One."
—Black Elk

Roman Pagan:
"The law imprinted on the hearts of all men is to love the members of society as themselves."
—Anonymous

Scientology: *"20: Try to treat others as you would want them to treat you."*
—L. Ron Hubbard

Shinto:
"Be charitable to all beings, love is the representative of God."
—Ko-ji-ki Hachiman Kasuga

Sikhism:
"Don't create enmity with anyone as God is within everyone."
—Guru Arjan Devji, 259

Sufism:
"The basis of Sufism is consideration of the hearts and feelings of others. If you haven't the will to gladden someone's heart, then at least beware lest you hurt someone's heart, for on our path, no sin exists but this."
—Dr. Javad Nurbakhsh, Master of the Nimatullahi Sufi Order

Taoism:
"Regard your neighbor's gain as your own gain, and your neighbor's loss as your own loss."
—T'ai Shang Kan Ying P'ien

Unitarian:
"We affirm and promote respect for the interdependent of all existence of which we are a part."
—Unitarian Principles

Wicca:
"An it harm none, do what thou wilt"
—The Wiccan Rede

Yoruba (Nigeria):
"One going to take a pointed stick to pinch a baby bird should first try it on himself to feel how it hurts."
—Anonymous

Zoroastrianism:
"Whatever is disagreeable to yourself do not do unto others."
—Shayast-na-Shayast 13:29

"To be one; to be united is a great thing. But to respect the right to be different is maybe even greater."

—Anonymous

Chapter Seven

Freedom of Space: Spacious Skies

This short story is about farmyard characters named Fluffy and Lucky who represent my wife and me. It emphasizes individuality in a relationship and following your creative instincts. Yes, I am the Lucky one having the time and space to explore my individual path. It helps to keep a loving and healthy relationship alive.

Once on a distant farmyard, there lived a kitty named Fluffy and a duckling named Lucky. They grew up together and soon became very close. In fact they grew to love each other and spent most of their time playing games and frolicking about.

Fluffy got her name from her beautiful fur coat and friendly personality. She would come up to many of the farm animals and purr delightfully. Sometimes she would even rub up to them at dinner time wanting to be petted and noticed. Fluffy became one of the most popular farmyard citizens.

In the meantime, Lucky received his name because most of the animals thought he was very "lucky" to have a kitty like Fluffy for a companion. Lucky duck soon grew into a wonderful mallard, aggressive and with a strong work ethic. He spent most of his time combing the weeds around the farmyard clearing bugs for the farmer, and the farmer was very pleased. However, Lucky worked so hard he failed to even notice when the other ducks and geese in the farmyard would head south for the winter. In fact, outside his life with Fluffy and work on the farm, he failed to notice many other things at all.

Several winters passed and every year it was the same. The other ducks on the farm would fly south and Lucky would stay to keep things in order and enjoy his life with Fluffy.

However, one winter finally swept in with the toughness of old man winter himself. The winds howled every night and cloudy coldness set in most of the days. Lucky started to have a tough time keeping up with his work. Something didn't quite seem the same. For deep inside, something was starting to brew. A numbing pain loomed like a large gaping sinkhole and the emptiness spread throughout. It was so unbearable Lucky had a hard time even getting out of bed. He had become a very unhappy duck that even Fluffy couldn't seem to cheer up.

As the days wore on, Lucky had an awakening. It was as if someone had snapped their fingers in his ear. He suddenly had a passion to fly south and join the other ducks. Although he tried to ignore these callings at first, they continued to haunt him almost everyday. This was totally new to him and he wasn't sure how to handle it. The urges soon got stronger and knocked him off balance. Lucky's work on the farm came to a crawl and he knew he needed to do something soon.

The idea of flying to uncertain lands by himself was more than a bit frightful. He sadly remembered his mother had once tried to fly south for the winter, only to get lost and confused. She was rescued only after spending time with the animal doctors in a faraway place. Lucky was still very sad because his mother later died at a very early age. Many of the animals thought this was why he was so fearful of flying with the other ducks.

The young Mallard was not used to taking fear as a partner, however, and often stood up to his fears around the farmyard. Reluctantly, he vowed to do this once again and told Fluffy of his desire to take wing to some faraway place. After all, what did he have to lose given his current condition?

Fluffy was very upset and couldn't understand why her mallard must leave. Was he that unhappy with her or with his life that he would want to leave her, even if it was just for the winter? She was worried he might get lost or injured and might not come back at all. She called him "self-centered" for wanting to leave. She sensed that this same little duckling she had grown up with all her life was slipping away and she didn't like it. She didn't want to see him change.

Lucky started to regret his decision to honor Fluffy's wishes. The fire and passion to fly south continued to burn bright. It was going to be a long winter. Even though the mallard loved his kitty very much, the sadness of not following his calling turned to anger. He sometimes would snap his bill at Fluffy, often for no apparent reason.

Fluffy could see something was wrong but dismissed it. You see, Lucky was so clever that around the farmyard he usually got his way. She saw it as the one time he wasn't getting his way. Meanwhile, she failed to see the flickering fire that was starting to smolder and burn deep within his soul.

Day after day, Lucky stumbled around the farmyard. The sadness of what he was missing, whatever strange thing that might be, was starting to tear him apart. The pain of longing for something unseen was not a physical pain; it seemed to pierce much deeper than that. He started to feel weak as if he was dying from the inside out. He tried to explain to Fluffy of the deep fire that burnt from within, but it was something hard to explain. When you are dying, those closest to you are often the last to know.

The farmer noticed Lucky's behavior and that his work was not up to par. He was not happy with what he saw. That combined with the winter's severity and a shortage of food prompted the farmer one day to come looking for the mallard, ax in hand.

The next day, Fluffy couldn't find Lucky. She looked throughout the farmyard and talked to the other animals. No one had seen him. She feared the worst. She just knew she had lost him forever.

Fluffy cried for days and wondered aimlessly around the farmyard. No other animal would ever take his place. She was sorry now that she had discouraged Lucky from taking his place among the flocks heading south. At least he would still be alive if he had followed his heart.

The bleakness of winter continued on and seemed to stretch forever. Fluffy did what she could to keep the mice out of the barn, but her work and heart were very heavy.

Then one bright Spring day Fluffy awoke to the tremendous rush and power of wings in flight. She looked heavenward and felt all the more sad as flock after flock passed over the farmyard on their return to the north. As she took her morning walk, wandering aimlessly as she so often did, she was engulfed by new warmth from within. Looking toward the horizon, she could see a beautiful mallard, wings slung back with flaps down for landing.

With much force, Lucky came swooshing into the middle of the farmyard! He waggled and quacked excitedly upon seeing Fluffy. The two pranced around in frenzy, as Lucky took the young feline into his wings in a happy embrace. His joy filled him like a balloon. He was happy again. He was content. Then he remembered the only thing in the world that could make him happier than seeing Fluffy.

It now came clearly what had urged him on toward his fearful path south. Traveling to faraway places had caused many stories to be written upon his heart and only now, after his long journey, could he begin to tell them.

Love is very patient and kind, never jealous
or envious, never boastful or proud, never
haughty or selfish or rude.

Love does not demand its own way. It is not
irritable or touchy. It does not hold grudges
and will hardly even notice when others
do it wrong.

It is never glad about injustice, but rejoices
whenever truth wins out.

If you love someone, you will be loyal to
her no matter what the cost. You will always
believe in her, always expect the best of her,
and always stand your ground
in defending her.

1 Corinthians 13:4-7

About the author

Harry Allen Strunk has been blessed with his wife Patty for 38 years and two great sons, Todger and Tanner (TJ). He is a third generation newspaper journalist and has worked for several daily newspapers, the Associated Press, and National Dragster magazine. Strunk's fiction stories delve into grief, gambling addiction, sexuality, Wall Street corruption, bipolar illness, and father-son conflicts. He has also published a poetry book on spirituality.

He has a seaplane commercial pilot's license and is a U.S. Coast Guard licensed captain. He splits his time living among the inspirational aspens of Colorado and the warmth and tranquility of the Florida Keys.

Strunk while working on Don Schumacher's Nitro Funny Car pit crew for his upcoming book, *Burning More Than Rubber.*

For more information:

www.aspengrovepublishing.com

NOTES . . .